Through Different Eyes

Mankiran Kaur

BookLeaf Publishing

India | USA | UK

Presentation by *BookLeaf Publishing*

Web: www.bookleafpub.com

E-mail: info@bookleafpub.com

ISBN: 9789363318151

First edition 2024

Solemnly, and (really), I dedicate this book and my work to all the readers out there trying to find a glimpse of beauty in this world and, through poetry, trying to find a glimpse of themselves. I dedicate this piece of my creation to the Almighty, who gave me enough strength to continue with creativity and add shimmer to everything. Or, in lyrical words: I am bejeweled to have experienced this experience and hope you will be too when you flip the pages...

ACKNOWLEDGEMENT

All the poems and the words are originally written. I look upon this great woman for her unbelievable skills in songwriting and poetry while encountering my journey through these words, thinking how much she had sacrificed and embraced every moment, thus remaining unmatched. (P.S. I am definitely talking about Taylor Swift). It's my pleasure to have written my work through all the words rotating in my mind, thus presenting you an "œuvre magnifique".

Moving on....

PREFACE

It is a great pleasure for me to introduce "Through Different Eyes." It incorporates the world through people's eyes and explains or explores the best of all worlds, and sometimes, the worst. Who am I kidding? We always fight between the best and the worst, like we're always trying to figure out who has passed the exam and who has not. Deliberately, but not. Unforeseen, but not. Literature is unique in its own way; let us embrace it, not judge it.

I shall always welcome suggestions from my sincere readers and the fairies hidden in between my words to improve and grow with this folklore.

Unnecessary but Necessary

When I am walking on the ground,
when everyone is about and around.

They shove cans and garbage with their feet,
Sometimes, I think I am a part of their fleet,
Thinking: "What's the point of Me?"

How much I try, how much I cry,
Don't come running, for this is not a fairytale,
not a lie.

Sometimes, we find it disturbing, knowing this:
When the others are acting,
we do this: act like we did not hear them but,
you know,
They expect you to;

That's what happens at parties,
When the mirrorball dances and rotates fro and
to, we do too.

Even though you know it too,
That,
this is not where you belong...
But, at the end of this folk song, will you know?
I don't think so.

Look at me, hidden between,
These words and telling,
You know what it is that you should or should
not know.

This world is not what you and I think.
But don't be thrown!
Be flown...
away and away, as much as you can,
from this throne...

Trust me, you do not want to know,
How they get after your worth and,
Cannot wait to watch the "aftershow".

The Road Taken

It is with great pleasure,
To this day, I measure...
My accomplishments.

Who was I if I was not me...
What could have I done,
If God did not show me…?

Wise men will always say...
Who follows them?
Those,
who ALREADY know their way.

"It's fine when it's not!
Everything's fine!
It's okay not to be okay!
It's worth trying!!"

I bet when you hear this,
You don't feel good, but worse,
It's like your whole life just changed its course…
Because it's engulfed in itself...
Not these phrases, trying to be praises.

My world is what I made it

Today and tomorrow, I choose it...
None of it matters if none of it matters to me...
Ghosts sitting beside me, believe me,
And so does their God...
Living for them is not in my dictionary,

But, continuously hearing this,
I CANNOT GET THEM OUT!!

My shelf is bejeweled with awards,
And so are my tears,
That is what I see and wanna hear...
The sounds of the struggle are now clear...
The road taken looks real.

Why Not...

...Change the meaning of a word?
I don't know… but
Here we go...

Can you define proverbs, though?
They are simply unimaginable, like,
Throwing your brain off the road!

To think that tackling the phrases was a man's
play,
But what about those that we learn EVERY
SINGLE DAY...?

Look closely and do see what to undermine,
for I am too this time,

"When life throws lemons, make lemonade."

Do you know that this is NOT our reality? We
are set out to soar, therefore,
When life throws lemons, we throw MORE and
MORE.
Time was right when it was, their minds were
right when they were...
It's all I can think about and go back that far,
Be real; we have come afar.
"All that glitters is not gold."

Why can we not let the glitter shine?
Why does gold always need to be so bright?
Why is my question thereby...

Therefore, proverbs do not define your life.
They are just a glimpse of time,
A glimpse of your future and what's behind.

Well, if you choose to stick to the age-old
definition that proverbs are mere words in a
mere list, then,
I think we are all surrounded by a blind mist.

Breathing is a Task

It's not often I write like this...
But when I do,
I'm taken away with a drift.

It's not nothing I watch every day,
But when I do,
I see the world, not blue but gray.

It's not magical until it's eradicated,
When it is,
All the kindness in the world is hated.

It's not sad anymore till it's panicking,

When the one whom you loved with all your
heart,
Set out for heaven.

It's not a wish anymore,
It's a desire,
To meet someday, someone who says:

"Dear child, from this life, you can retire."

It's important till it's undone,
It's urgent till there's not one,
But urgency, it's not a 'need', do you mind,
till one of us succumbs...
Well, what can I say,
That's life!
sigh That's life...

The New Beginner

Did you hear about that girl,
whose world set out to be fake,
That girl who worked hard for a change of fate?

Did you hear about that girl who, never mind,
never stayed?
It's not personal till it got for her that way,
"It's fine…," she said,
got blue and black and bled.

But now she soared!
In between and up,
Heaven and hell,
Her voice reaches everywhere and to every soul.

Let me rephrase,
For I lost the pathway,
She is still on her way,
Her voice reaches through and out every soul.

I was waiting,
I was a keen kid,
I was wearing her lyrics on my sweatshirt, I
STILL AM.

Reminiscing what she mended for me,
I STILL AM.
Loved how it started and lived how it ended, I
STILL AM.

Her dark side blended,
when her folklore ended,
when her friends befriended,
when her pink and golden caged,
IT STILL IS.

But she never bended
To sorrow, to hate, to escape,
She stayed!
Still does, even in her gray.

That's my role model!
What can I say,
She's Legendary,

Selling records every day!
ThankYou, Taytay♡

The Difference between the Creator and his Creations

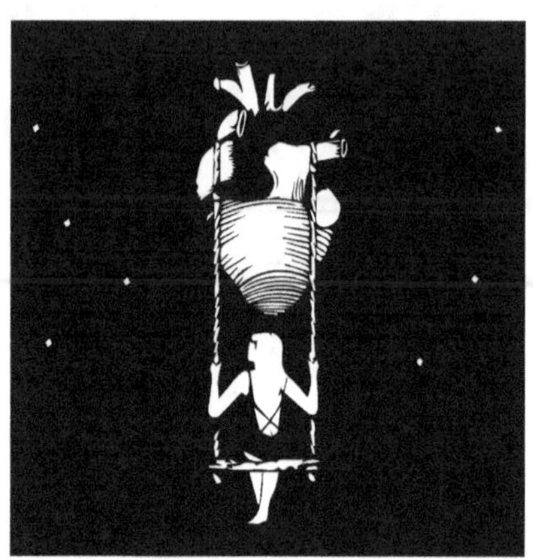

Have we not met before?
Or maybe I forgot.

Have we not let our souls go?
Or maybe I forgot.

Every time there's drama, there's karma.
One side is wrong, who knows the other is right?
God.

When you're down on your feet, begging,
Who knows for you, who's gonna fight?
God.

Every time I see his creations walking by,
making me uncomfortably uncontrollable.
Seeing their petty ideas and petty minds,
Reminding me to speak these lines.
I cannot. But I wrote them in my mind.
Who reads that?
God.

They don't know how much he sacrificed for,
what he sacrificed for
This World, that you call YOURS.

That's why, sometimes, I'm sorry for how great
he is and us, his creations are not.
That's why, sometimes, I feel boring,
That my friend is so far away from me,
Yet near.

It's heartbreaking to watch such a human soul,
being inhuman.
Shouldn't be like this,
God.

[Yes, it shouldn't be like this...]

Enid Blyton's Bedtime Bookshelf

It is quite clear,
How we can't bear,
Every single tortured scar that keeps rotating
from arm to hair,
Like lines going above in a science experiment.
Please!
It has never not been not irrelevant.

It has meaning, our dreams and our lives both.
Just like Enid Blyton's Bedtime Bookshelf,
Beyond the bearing benefits humans have in
store.

When the six red wizards weren't able to get in
through the door,

Who am I or who are you, who doesn't even
have witchcraft to start with,
And end this searing soar.

Why do you need to end. It?
My mind just keeps revolving around these
beneficial benefits that you are freely wasting
around, don't soar!
But get bored!

At least, the characters know their character.
Doesn't matter how witty they are,
They know their competitors, their creators and
all the fairy Godmothers.
Thank God!

We are not in Enid Blyton's Bedtime Bookshelf,
Or else,
We wouldn't be able to play our characters,
Let alone,
A heart full of adventure and danger.
We couldn't be able to face the betrayal,
Let alone,
A ready-made world waiting for the admired.
We are doing great,
but Enid Blyton's Bedtime Bookshelf is the
greatest.

Insight Inside

Me, myself and I,
Heard this song before,
Never heard its meaning.

Heard these words before,
Never hear yourself.

How much would you run?
To become "the one?"
It's not in your hands,
leave it.
But don't succumb and,
Fall back

Not today, but...
Why am I seeing this damaged raft?
Went inside, saw a magnifique craft!

Why am I seeing Glitters and Gold?
Went inside,
Now I'm blind. But I'm bold.

Why am I seeing this playful project?
Lying there, all alone,
just cobwebs.

Why am I seeing this beautiful, lifeless life?
In a random ship which said Goodbye.

Too soon,
No route,
Sank below,
My room.

Heart smashed,
The beauty queen died,
Her life lacked,
In front of my eyes.

Gold below the sea,
The living died,
Non-living stayed and stated:
"I think now their statements are exemplified."

What did I do?
I let the gold stay where it wants to,

I let the beauty stay within what it haunts to,
I let the glitter shine however it wants to,
No sign of insane humans there on the ship, but I said
Goodbye to,
The shining within...

Have you Thought about Thoughts?

Not appropriate but here it goes,
Not today, but for tomorrow,
Which may never come,
And still, today never goes by...

(Quite interesting!)

Have to have this, not that,
Don't mention that!
That's that!

(Quite meaningless)

There goes their heir!
Driving flawlessly like her hair,
Are they acting!
By the way, who knows if they're!

(Quite confusing!)

I hate to be true,
But this IS the truth.
It's not magical always,
Until these words get in your own way,
What about them? They,
They will always say.
However, it's you who must tell them,
"It's MY day!" with a smile anyway.

Unrealistic wants, wants Real?

"The world will always want,"
What?
Of course, what YOU want!

"It's urgent!"
Not at all,
Their brain is telling them,
not to be unrealistic!

We're servants of the one who cares,
Who never dares,
Infact bewares and like, always awares.
So what's the point of being a "connoisseur"
who never REALLY cares...?

Just spitting facts all day,
No matter what you say,

It'll always be them, you know, whom YOU
ALWAYS BLAME...

Maybe it's time to see,
Who wins reality?
Unrealistic wants, one day, will it be "I want
Me!"...?
I hope so, but that day,
Maybe I'll never live to see...

Oh! It's That Memory...

Here to tell the truth,
What most kids don't,
Don't mind if I do,
I want you to not get stuck.

In between the lines, cause they're always
hidden?!
Bites me, even though I don't have a kitten...

I wanted them to breathe...
But seeing their sacrifice,
I couldn't realise how much they missed their
sea.

Those fishes, that I still reminisce,
Have I been reminded of their bliss?
Their eyes, that might not have been pleasing to
me,
But seeing life in a box of water at my home,
was never not intimidating...

For me! I was really happy.
But the day I did not see them,
I don't remember that, but remember feeling
sorry,
Gloomy,
Realising their fish food still made itself to our
home, with no one to eat that.
It was unruly, truly.

Life doesn't get a Perfect Match...

Unless it's Death.
But I don't wanna discover...
What lies ahead...
I don't wanna find...
But I Do!!

I have theories,
Told by my family's family,
It's not unholy,
It's just extravagantly
Extravagant!

Don't bother...
Death will come slowly unless you wander
The dark woods will lead you to that dark
brother!
But it's another and then another.

I get terrified when that message is shared,

To the friends and family who cared and still
care,
But I don't think I can ever remove that portrait
stare.

It's just that… that I wish for a beautiful
afterlife,
But seeing deathly invitations, all white,
I prefer God giving me signs,
In this life,

That he made so beautifully,
It's not unholy,
It's all floral and beautiful and deserving!
For me, myself and I who are writing and him
who is speaking.
It's all good,
Just.
Stay.
Like.
This.
Don't die.
Bye!

Forgive but Never Forget

There's a reason for my enrollment,
Participating everywhere.
It's not "showing off"
I have an interest in some interesting interests.

It's an exam till it's not,
Till there's time to prepare,
Then there's not,
Then everywhere, there's chaos.

Because it's their behavior!
Peeking into other's papers!
It's their habit!
Of trying to get all of the info from your friend
with whom you promised "long-lasting
friendship."

"It's obviously not not fair"
For me, it is unfair.
It's eradicated memories
But I remember even a millisecond of all
tragedies.

It'd not been true if it had been you!
Not being for the one who won,
But being there for the one whom you expected
to...
Because IT'S ALWAYS YOU!

Those successful souls who don't get admired,
I'm writing with regret but revenge within veins
rushing,
Why's it always us, that's us, who, through these
crowds, are pacing...?

Well, I guess, it's part of the process,
This racing,
It's just saving,
Our own souls,
And even they are thriving!

When the Power goes OFF!!

Good call!
How's now the time you choose?
Come on! Don't be late; I can only think about
cold water and cold winds flowing through this
summer gate...
But seeing you run away like this, makes me
anticipate...

If you will come or not,
When the power goes off.

It is quite quiet everywhere,
Seeing dark right now is making me not go
anywhere,
Just to my cold, icy dreams, which make my
mind go places rare,
But please, power, don't snare...

Don't snarl at the people, even if you want to,
I AGREE WITH YOU, because I ALWAYS
KNEW.
That one day, even nature will turn against us,
because it's not full of surprises,
That we're stuck in a midnight midtown bus.

Well! Thank GOD and YOU,
When the power goes off,
Everyone everywhere, obviously tells truthful
truths,
Don't you worry, they'll not fulfil them,
I know you know,
THIS IS THE TRUTH...
sigh When the power goes off.

I don't and I won't and I can't

Not right now,
But I use this phrase,
Definitely in my mind,
Obviously, out of craze.

Not now, not then and never,
Did I shout this in front of anyone,
Seeing the circumstances,
And the consequences,
I wanted to, but I was out on my own run.

I wish to speak to,
About if I can redo,
Everything I think about, and every truth,
That sinks in the quicksand in my mind,
So fast, that it gets out of line.

I think and I'm thinking,

What if I say this phrase,
And everyone calls me rude?
But it's the TRUTH.

Maybe it's too much
Thinking,
Blinking,
And
Crinkling of the eye,
That it started wrinkling.

It's not always a sacrifice that you're not
welcoming,
It's not always heartbreaking,
It might be that you're just relating...

And I'm just being.

I don't and I won't and I can't
Be like anything you are.
I don't and I won't and I can't
Copy everything you do, like that hidden snarl;
I don't and I won't and I can't
Read your mind, thinking what you are.
I don't and I won't and I can't
Abandon my path and step onto cobwebs,
leading myself to scars.

there will always be Hate for those who Love

I tried,
So many times,
When my heart died,
I cried.
And cried.
And so I,
Stopped.

Believing in the so-called believers,
I stopped.
Living in their world like I am a hungry beaver,
So I stopped.
Giving mine to them,
I stopped
Laughing at those silly dares.
I stopped.

Because it's starting to scare,
Getting scared, being unaware,
That the ones you love so much,
Are the ones who text you rare, and they stare
with that uneasy glare.

Maybe, it's time, I leave this bliss,

Which is for them,
but for me, I will never miss.

It's that alarming,
That even your ears can't handle.
It's that harming,
That with every bad wind, their sound breaks out
your candle.

It's not often times this happens,
In my mind and that mobile device,
my brain disappears when my tears appear.

I know I know I know,
That, Pain is what makes you grow,
But haven't you thought about those?
Who gave their everything, and they rose,
So good, so bad, yet still,
it's always less than "that."

I hope,
I'm not the only one,
Cause I won!
But still,
Cannot find anywhere to run.

Mind-blowing, God-gifting Happiness!

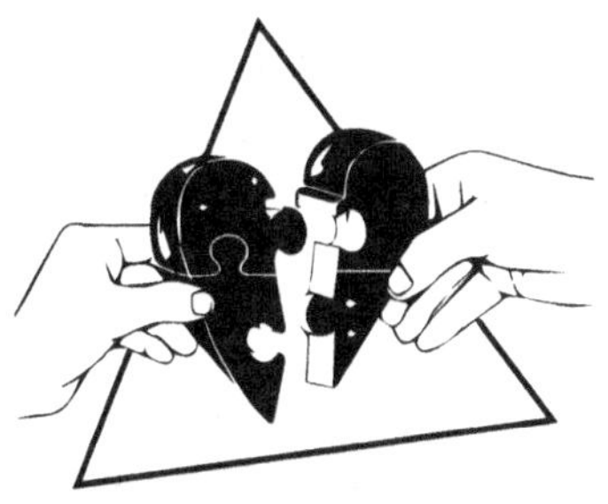

"I assume it belongs to the one,
They put golden and silver rings on,
That's the closest I've come,
To my heart exploding."

Someone said this,
And I messed it,
In my mind, when I guessed it,
I thought one thought,
thinking what's true, what's not.

One-time thinking,
That blinking is your truest enemy,
Have you not been crinkling,
When it is quiet, is it necessary?

I'd picked up myself then and there,
When I stared,

Right into the eyes of happiness,
Knocking the door, if it was even there...

However, it's very rare...
Having to build up happiness up the stairs,
I've seen many with tears, not for crying but for
winning gold medals, which they forever handle
with care...

Now, that's something… to be proud of,
For I never knew that even once, to be honest,
That this is what makes the crowd,
Of cement that never steals our knowledge.

For I long for that Mind-blowing, God-gifting
happiness,
Which I know to get, will cause me distress.
But not everyone assumes it,
They work to breathe it.

It's all about Importance, till there's None left.

"That person!
Won!
My!
Heart!!"

Was there even an explanatory explanation?
Or just a coincidence?
Did you think before you thought about that
person?
Or just a luck-caused incident?
Was it too soon when they lost?
Or were they your curses or well-wishes?
Was it not humanity that you fought for?
Or just a past-no good best friend?
Fine!
You won, they lost.

But shouldn't you be the one who must be filled
with humbleness?
Shouldn't you be the one who should support the
lost fortress?
Shouldn't you be the one to scream, even in this
distress?
Shouldn't you be "the one?"

I think that even I don't have answers to these
questions,
For it's true,
It's all about Importance, till there's none left.
It's all about That Person,
Till today,
Then tomorrow another comes,
Replaced and Replaced,
So, you see, that's why I guess,
They say, Tomorrow Never Comes, why?
It gets replaced by Today.

No, Not, and Never

Quite a confusion, they've caused!
Drowned in illusion, am I?
Then I guess I'm lost.

Helping me get up won't do!
But can you bring me a waffle?
Dipped in chocolate Belgian, that too!
Yes! Exactly! This world is a falafel.

God! How fed up am I?
Of this "No and Not and Never?"
People say this with a cry!
But just till they see this phrase and realize why!

Not everything and everyone has meaning,

What if I told you this,
With a Never and a No and a Not and If?
AS IF!
Why's it rotating in my mind?
This world, that too, in rewind?
I pray and crave,
For this No, and Not and Never,
To leave MY GRAVE.

For you see,
It's me,
Behind the scenes,
Saying this secretly,
To the people who I don't want to talk to, really.

Up that Rollercoaster!

It's here,
The level of frustration,
You can't bear.

"When it's emotionally investing,
It's giving away yourself.
Time doesn't know how old you are.
You put meaning to it.
It's interesting.
It's not.
Haven't done with old books?
Don't throw them, read them."

How does it feel to listen to constant reminders
on your phone?
Feels like frustration hasn't even gone up that
throne..

It's not you till you do it
Faking it till you make it, is your bullet.
You just graze it, no questions asked.

Having to crave cake after every important task?
Does your reminder remind you to feed, to sleep
or be uneasy while, of course, watching TV!

It's random to think about randomness.
However, if you're dancing on your beat,
Why care about others' feet??

It'd be best for you to let yourself fleet.
Have good beef and say Good Night to your
own sleep.

That's a real roller-coaster,
not the reminders we get reminded of, daily.

I wandered lonely as a Folk Song

I wandered lonely as a folk song,
If anyone would want to listen,
The times have got transferred into the wrong,
But here, I am, like always, just glistens.

I wandered lonely as a folk song,
Just to pass from one ear to another,
Hoping to get picked up from,
Graves of those who loved to wither.

I wandered lonely as a folk song,
Wondering if I have the courage to change my
taste,
Not back then, but now, I think this world will
not let me be safe.
I wandered lonely as a folk song,

With my mind, not fit for this music range.

I wandered lonely as a sad song,
Straight out from the files of an old folklore,
Hoping to soar,
But when I entered this world,
I never knew that I would get replaced by
another verse...